BAD DAD

BAD DAD

A Guide to Pitiful Parenting

TOM COTTER

Willow Street Press New York

PROLOGUE: A BAD DAD'S WORDS OF WISDOM

This book is all about child-rearing, which sounds disturbingly wrong. You should never "rear" a child.

Okay, let me start again...

This book is a satirical mockery of fatherhood, and lampooning parenthood in general. Please take what I have written with a grain of salt, unless you are a diabetic. If you are a born-again Christian, or a devout Muslim, please close the book, place it down on a flat surface and back away slowly. Please do not take any of my advice literally. Like the term "baby sitting," it is not to be taken literally. It is morally and ethically wrong to sit on a baby, and it is illegal in several states.

Any following of the advice contained within this book, without the expressed written consent of Tom Cotter or Major League Baseball, is strictly prohibited.

Do not attempt to read this book if you are elderly, or pregnant, or God forbid both, which is nasty. Do not operate heavy machinery while reading this book.

Most importantly, if you are easily offended, please close the book now, and store it in a warm and dry place for your next book burning. If you enjoy this book, the author's name is Tom Cotter. If you did not enjoy the book, my name is Salman Rushdie.

In my stand-up, I talk a great deal about my fictitious father:

My dad was a "Foster Parent." That's what he drank, Fosters.

My father and I have been butting heads since I was in the womb.

When I was a small child, my dad would kiss me on the lips, until one day I slipped him the tongue. Now, he won't even shake my hand. I'll never forget that Halloween, when he dressed me up like a dog and left me outside of a Korean restaurant. What a kidder Dad was. When I graduated from college, my father tried to surprise me with a car, but he missed. Okay, none of that is true.

The fact is that my dad is a truly remarkable man, and everything I learned about fatherhood, I learned from the best...I learned from him. He served in the South Pacific during WWII, and upon his return, he put himself through college and medical school, en route to becoming a brilliant neurosurgeon, devoted husband and father of six children. I am the runt of that litter. He is unbelievably generous and, without question, the most intelligent man that I have ever known. He worked ridiculous and exhausting hours — not only to provide for his family — but to ensure that we attended the finest private schools and colleges because he placed such a high value on education. Imagine how thrilled he was when his youngest decided to use that expensive education to tell jokes to drunks in bars for a living. Despite that devastating disappointment, he has always been supportive of my siblings and me, no matter what paths we have chosen for our own lives, and he inspires me to be a better man by his example. And so I dedicate this book to Dr. Walter Cornelius Cotter.

Lastly, I would be remiss if I didn't mention my bride, Kerri Louise, and by "remiss" I mean punished, both physically and emotionally. The fact is, she is not only the mother of my children, but a far better parent than I could ever be. She has given me the greatest gift of all in my children and, although there are times that I wish I had the receipt, I can't imagine taking this journey without her by my side. I urge you to check out her upcoming book (right after you read this one) and her webisodes on motherhood at www.mymommyminute.com.

Put your child on your shoulders and jump up and down...directly under the ceiling fan.

IT TAKES A VILLAGE IDIOT

The future may be bright, but genetics assure that your children won't be.

~

The best classroom in the world is at the feet of an elderly person. It's also one of the smelliest classrooms.

~

Teach your child the Metric System through your cocaine addiction.

~

Your son is one in a million, which means in China, there are 10,000 just like him.

~

Teach your children that honey attracts more flies than vinegar, but dog poo and corpses generally attract the most.

~

To ensure academic success, you must push your child. Punching and kicking are also very effective.

~

A low cost alternative to the game *Operation* can be had with a fork and an electric socket.

~

Kids are naturally inquisitive, and they have a yearning to learn, so remember that there are no stupid questions, just annoying children.

~

Inform your child that life is a series of hurdles, and his legs are too short to be a hurdler, so he is doomed to fail.

~

Encourage your child to be the "teacher's pet," and give the teacher written authorization to have him neutered.

~

Today's class clown is tomorrow's valedictorian… but probably at clown college.

~

Make certain that your daughter is on the Honor Roll, and not having boys rolling on her.

~

Tell your son that it's wrong to peek over some-one's shoulder during a test. Especially if it's a urine test.

~

Art can be exciting. Draw a chalk outline around the homeless man on the sidewalk.

~

Have a water balloon fight, but put yours in the freezer the night before to assure victory.

~

There is nothing more fun than clowning around with your little Rascal. You know, the scooter you stole from that elderly man at the mall.

~

Teach your son how to burn an ant with a magnifying glass, then teach him how to burn an uncle with an acetylene torch.

~

Grab some shovels and dig for treasure with your son. Start at a local cemetery.

~

Play *Duck, Duck Goose* with your children. It teaches them discrimination. It sucks to be the goose.

~

Help your daughter with her science project, but get really high first.

~

Sponsor an underprivileged child in Africa. Have your kids write to him and establish a relationship. Use discretion when he is ultimately eaten by hyenas.

~೨

You can develop your child's finger dexterity by building mini paper airplanes, using rolling papers.

~೨

Seven is an ideal age to teach your son about the birds and the BB guns.

~೨

Build sandcastles with your child in a miniature, indoor sandbox but get out of the way when the cat has to poop.

~೨

Take your kids to the library...maybe the Librarian can get them to shut the hell up.

~

Play *Hide & Seek* with your child, and rest assured that he won't find you because you have to be 21 to get into a titty bar.

~

Encourage your children to sing in the car. It makes time go by faster and it annoys the hell out of cab drivers.

~

Let your child retrieve your mail from the mailbox. He will experience a sense of accomplishment, and kids have no idea what a letter bomb looks like.

~

Write a series of children's mystery novels about lactose intolerant, gaseous brothers called *The Farty Boys*.

～

Buy your son a BB gun, and take him outside to shoot at cans...Mexi-cans, Puerto Ri-cans, Domini-cans, because you are a Republi-can.

～

Put your child in your lap, and let him steer the car on the way home from Thanksgiving. That way, technically, you are not driving while intoxicated.

～

Take your overweight child to a heavy petting zoo.

～

Sing to your children, so that they may develop a hatred for karaoke.

~

If your child is a tattletale, handle it exactly as the Mafia would.

~

Never give an epileptic child an Etch-a-Sketch. It's cruel.

~

Get deeply involved with your child's school life, by sleeping with his teacher.

~

Coach your son's soccer team, and if he is the weak link, do the right thing for the team, and trade him to another team.

~

1. Blindfold your child and hand him a stick.
2. Position him in front of the beehive in the back yard.
3. Yell "Piñata" and run like hell.

~

Take your kids to a Wiggles concert. Light a joint, and start a mosh pit.

~

Potato sack races are frowned upon on St. Patrick's Day.

~

Teach your daughter how to dance.
Install a pole in her playroom.

HAZING, I MEAN RAISING A CHILD

Take your son to a parade. More specifically, the Gay Pride Parade. The follow-up questions are priceless.

~

Nothing amps up a squirt gun fight like filling them with bleach.

~

Teach your child the correct way to handle fireworks. Then high five him with your hook hand.

~

Chop down a cherry tree with your son. Then lie about it.

~

Go cow tipping with your son, but don't get out of the car. It's less messy that way. For added fun, invite one of his Hindu classmates along.

~

If you want your child to sleep, sing to her. If you want her to cry, try rapping.

~

Having a child fall asleep in your arms is one of the most peaceful feelings in the world. Make sure you discard the ether rag and rubber gloves properly.

~

If you need your baby to wake up, just start making love to your wife. It works every time.

~

Tell your children to sleep tight, and make it so —
with a straight jacket and bungee cords.

~

Playing darts with a hemophiliac child really rais-
es the stakes.

~

Remember the three "P"s when potty training:
Patience, Practice & Pitchfork.

~

Play army with your son…at the Salvation Army.

~

When your toddler is having a tantrum, a nap may be in order. He will calm down way before you wake up.

~

If your child falls asleep in the middle of a bed-time story, it's probably your boring delivery.

~

Create a CD of rain or waves to help your child sleep. Once asleep, dump a bucket of water on his face.

~

True serenity can be felt just by putting your children to sleep. They call it "euthanasia", but it works on the youth in North America, too.

~

When you reprimand your child, do not raise your voice. Use more of a creepy whisper.

~

Getting into hot water can be a good thing, because it sanitizes the filthy little brat.

~

You never have to hit your child, thanks to modern parenting techniques and the invention of the Taser.

~

When you are angry at your child, go off to a quiet area, by yourself, and take a series of deep breaths...through a bong.

~

Teach your children that they live in a democracy where the rights of the individual are valued and cherished; however they also live in your house, which is a brutal dictatorship that believes in torture and slavery.

~

When your child misbehaves, show him his birth certificate, and the expiration date that you added.

~

If your son is struggling at Little League baseball, remember "pinch hitting." Your wife should pinch him while you hit him. That'll learn him.

~

If your child is a pain in the ass, make him feel a pain in the ass.

~

Give your child choices:
Choice # 1…Clothes in hamper.
Choice #2…Foot in ass.

~

Spankings and time outs may be unpleasant when you are 10, but they will be cherished after 30.

~

When Chris Rock was a child, and his parents gave him a spanking, they were hitting Rock bottom.

~

Never hold a baby above your head after he has eaten.

~

Be a grown-up. It's hard to discipline your child when you are both wearing the same Batman shirt.

~

Parents should work as a team. "Just wait till your father gets home…He'll be right back from going out to get cigarettes seventeen years ago. He'll be here any minute now."

~

You want your children to have principles. Principals that will hold them down while their teachers beat them into submission.

~

Punish with a loving heart. You can get one from the city morgue.

~

When your child says "I hate you!" respond with "I love you!" while forcing his head back into the toilet.

~

If your child asks if onions are the only vegetable that can make you cry, say "no" and then beat him with a cucumber.

~

You should never hit your child when you are angry. Wait until you are in a really good mood and then whack the shit out of him. It'll keep him on his toes.

~

Once you have a baby, you will never again sleep like one.

~

If your child is angry with you, don't be afraid to say, "I'm sorry...I'm sorry that you were ever born."

~

Fill your child with Joy by making him drink dishwashing liquid. He probably won't swear again after that.

~

If you want to torture your pets, buy your three-year-old son a whistle.

~

Start every bedtime story with: "Once upon a time there was a handsome prince named DADDY and an evil witch named MOMMY..."

~

Help your son write a letter to Santa. Start the letter with "Dear Fat Fuck…"

FATHER FAILURES

It's hard to tell your son not to pull hair when his Mommy can be heard begging for it in a loud passionate voice late at night.

~

Buy your whiny child a pet to cuddle with like a porcupine or a rattle snake.

~

Introduce your child to wonders of French cuisine, by cutting off his pet frog's legs and eating them in front of him.

~

Teach your child that words can hurt, by beating him with a dictionary.

~

If your daughter complains that she never had a pet to sleep with, gently remind her of the two dozen adorable head lice she had for the better part of last summer.

～

Introduce your child to the wonders of chemistry by starting a meth lab.

～

It's difficult to raise a morbidly obese child, and it's more difficult to raise one over your head.

～

Never give your child a laxative and a sleeping pill at the same time.

～

Childhood enthusiasm is a wonder to behold, and it can be controlled through Ritalin or restraints.

～

Nothing spices up a birthday party like playing *Pin the Tail on the Donkey* with a live donkey.

～

If you think there is good in every child, you haven't met Every Child.

～

When Pampers puts "Good for up to 24 lbs." on the box of diapers, they are not talking about the weight of the poo.

～

Bounce your baby boy on your knee. Not all of him, just his head… like a soccer ball. Infants love that.

～

Monitor your child's temperature daily, with a rectal thermometer. This will not only gauge his overall health but it will also clearly establish that you are the boss.

～

Don't throw the baby out with the bathwater — but if you do, snake the pipes right away.

～

Multicultural babies are so beautiful and yet so embarrassing to their grandparents.

～

There is nothing more devastating than losing a child…in a poker game.

～

Lifting your son up to use the "big boy" urinal is fine, unless he is 17. Then it's the reason mall security has been summoned.

～

When your child has the chicken pox, you can't be too careful. Wear a HAZMAT suit and feed him with a slingshot.

～

There is nothing stronger than the bond between a mother and her child, especially when Krazy Glue is involved.

～

Put your child's school picture on the refrigerator door. Tell him it's because you are trying to lose weight and his face makes you lose your appetite.

~

Assure your child that his scrapes, bumps and bruises will all heal, and he will be as good as new. However, what he did to Mommy during child birth was so severe that her boo boo will never be as good as new again.

~

Teach your children to welcome change by forcing them to beg for it, in the subway.

~

"Hugs, not drugs" – they are not mutually exclusive. In fact, sometimes they go really well together.

~

When your child asks what a vagina is, tell him it's another word for your nose, then sit back and laugh at phrases like, "My teacher caught me picking my vagina in class today" and "My principal has a huge vagina."

~

Tell your son that he is a descendant of Adam and Eve and if he asks if we evolved from apes say, "No, that's your mother's side of the family."

~

When they complain about the taste of cough syrup, explain that Daddy doesn't like the taste of Tequila either but he drinks it every day without whining like a bitch.

~

Teach your child about King Arthur and Excalibur, by Krazy Gluing his toys to the floor.

~

Leave your toddler alone with a box of Crayola crayons, and the next day he will poop a magic rainbow.

~

Encourage your children to read in the car by texting while you drive.

~

Tell your son that some children have grandparents and some really lucky children have great-grandparents, but his are just average.

~

Buy your children some gold fish for their aquarium. The crackers, not the real ones, silly.

~

On Halloween, dress your child up as a Jehovah's Witness, and then laugh as nobody answers the door for him.

~

For one dollar a day, or $30 per month, you can sponsor a starving child in Africa. Or for the same $30, you can get all the premium cable channels. That's a no brainer.

~

Tell your child that the clay pottery bowl he made in art class is the most beautiful thing that you've ever seen — and then use it as an ashtray.

~

If your child is adopted and your walls are thin, try not to yell out, "Who's your Daddy?" during sex.

~

When your child whines that she wants to go to the beach, agree to take her after she watches an instructional video on beach safety called Jaws.

~

Teach your child the joy of sharing by making her donate a kidney.

~

Teach your son to never take "no" for an answer, especially when he is on a date.

~

Children's car safety seats are expensive.
Duct tape is cheap. Just sayin'.

DADDY DON'TS

.

Inform your child that eating your boogers is wrong…unless you've just snorted cocaine. Then it's just frugal.

~

Help your son score with the ladies by building up his immunity to mace.

~

For Christmas, give your son an air guitar. If he complains, tell him that you can't return it because you lost the air receipt.

~

History can be fun. Teach your child about Ben Franklin by having him fly a kite under high voltage lines.

~

Teach your child to open his heart to others. Tell him to use a sterilized scalpel and a local anesthesia.

~

Warn your children about the hazards of smoking. Tell them that cigarettes don't make you look cool. They do, however, make you look sexy. Very, very sexy.

~

Tell your son that God gave him two of almost everything. Two eyes, two ears, two legs, two lungs, two nostrils, two testicles, but only one penis — so he should hold on to that penis really tight.

~

Teach your child that honesty is the best policy, but the "No Smoking" policy is a violation of personal freedom.

~

Every child should feel significant, important and wanted, so it's best to hide your wife's addiction to the morning after pill.

~

Never allow your children to play *Twister* in a trailer park. It's bad karma.

~

Leave a deep impression on your son. Right behind his ear, under the hair line, where his teachers won't see it.

~

If you live near cannibals, never refer to your son as "butter fingers" or your daughter as "sweet heart."

~

Tell your son that he has "privates"...but Daddy has "Generals."

~

Teach your child the joy of giving to the poor. By "giving" of course I mean the finger.

~

Tell your son that today, you are digging a hole to China in the back yard, and his dog "Rusty" is just napping under the sheet next to the hole.

~

Teach your children to respect their elders because where there is a will, there is an inheritance.

~

Many married couples argue and fight after their child's birthday party. It usually starts when you notice the clown makeup on your wife's inner thigh.

~

Display your child's drawings on the refrigerator door…on the inside.

~

Teach your youngest child that if he wants the good piece of chicken at dinner, he'll have to spit on it. It's called "marking your territory."

~

Assure your children that when Mommy & Daddy are fighting, it's probably all their fault.

~

Encouragement from a teacher can turn a student's life around, but electroshock therapy can do it much faster.

~

Children should listen closely to their grandparents because they have experience and wisdom, and because the dementia and Alzheimer's make their stories kind of fun.

~

You are your child's most important teacher, and ironically, his least favorite.

~

Impress upon your children that they should listen to your advice, and ignore your example.

~

Teach your kids that bigger is not always better, especially in regard to tumors.

~

It's harmful for parents to live out their athletic fantasies through their children. Maybe your little princess doesn't want to be a nose tackle...Let it go.

~

You'll find what you need in the arms of a child. Type "O" negative blood.

~

Tell your son that if he tells the school nurse that his wing-ding hurts, she has to take a look at it. Those are the rules, and he should use them to his advantage.

~

Your teenage son is a handsome idiot. I'm just kidding. He is not handsome at all.

~

Teach your teen that Joy is contagious, so he should wash his hands after he feels her up.

~

Your children will have you in stitches...because they hate hearing "no," and they are remarkably skilled with box-cutters.

~

When you are cooking, let your child lick the spoon, but only after it has cooled from heating up your heroin.

~

Your child should know that sometimes love hurts…especially in prison.

~

Your child may need braces — a neck brace, a knee brace, a back brace — and you may need some Anger Management classes.

~

Tell your teenage son that people often judge you by the company you keep, and his company is "Massengill" because he is a category 4 douche.

~

Teach your daughter to be open to new things. Her mind, not her legs.

~

Children should make small decisions with their head, and big decisions with their heart...and they should make huge decisions with their lawyer.

~

What a child learns at home lasts until the grave, which could be tomorrow, if he can't keep his big mouth shut.

~

You can say, "It's just a phase" all you want, but the reality is that you have given birth to a douche bag.

~

Hug a teacher. While you're at it, feel up a principal and goose a lunch lady.

~

Tell your kids that they should write
their names on everything they own with
permanent ink…and start with the cat.

STUFF THEY WILL WORK OUT IN THERAPY

No need to worry about teen pregnancy. Your daughter's personality is a highly effective form of birth control.

~

Brush your teenage daughter's hair, but use the dog grooming brush. If she asks why, tell her it's because she is an insufferable bitch.

~

Your pre-mature daughter spent months in an incubator, and now look at her. She is radiant, in a mutant radioactive sort of way.

~

Be warned. After your baby is born you will have to endure the "Terrible Two's"…your wife and her mother.

~

Alcohol consumption during pregnancy can cause low fetal birth weight, so drink heavily and you'll have no trouble shitting that baby out.

~

Girls and boys mature differently. Girls usually finish puberty by age 15, and boys usually finish by age 50.

~

Children grow like weeds and, trust me, there will be days that you wish you had some weed killer.

~

"Adolescent" contains the word "scent" which is appropriate because your kid will start to stink right about then.

~

Fear not. If all of your son's friends jumped off of a bridge, he wouldn't — because your son is a pussy.

~

You want your son to have faith, but you want him to wear a condom because Faith is the neighborhood skank.

~

Tell your child to look both ways before crossing the street...up and down.

~

Give a child some fish, and he'll eat for a day. Teach a child to fish, and he'll grow up to beat his wife.

~

Teach your children that "cooties" are just the on-set of Ebola.

~

Make your child feel special, by making him wear a hockey helmet in public. Tell him it's a crown and he is a prince, and it's why daddy can park anywhere.

~

Teach your child the joy of stamp collecting...by buying your groceries with food stamps.

~

Warn your children that they can't hide their sorrows, but they can hide their mashed potatoes in a glass of milk.

~

Teach your child how to identify Poison Ivy, then teach him how to rub his camp counselor's boxers in it.

~

A parent should always try to be in good spirits, which is easier if good spirits are always in the parent.

~

Warn your teenage daughter that nothing in life comes easy, except a 17-year-old boy.

~

Warn your son that the ache of unfulfilled dreams is the worst pain of all. Unless you accidentally put Gold Bond medicated powder on your scrotum.

~

Explain to your child that it doesn't cost anything to be nice, but being mean is also free.

~

Having a baby doesn't solve marital problems, but it does give you someone else to hate.

~

As a parent, you must keep faith alive. That way you are more likely to get the ransom money from Faith's parents.

~

A mother is always happy to see her son, except when she is watching gay porn.

~

A baby monitor allows you to listen in on the angelic first words of your infant, and the satanic curse words of your wife.

~

If your child is upset, she'll calm down much sooner if you are calm. So, calmly collect her severed fingers off the ground, slowly back away from the Rottweiler, and gingerly walk her to the hospital pointing out the pretty flowers along the way.

~

Dress up like a pirate and tell your kids that you want to get your hands on their booty...no, wait. Don't say that.

~

You view other people's children in a whole new light when you have one of your own. Their children are inferior, and destined to fail.

~

Even if you move 1000 miles away, your mother still tells you what to do, and you still feel compelled to do it. This is especially true when she is holding your daughter hostage, and those are the ransom demands.

~

The day your child finally spreads his wings is the day you realize that you have fathered some kind of mutant Bird-boy. You shouldn't have fucked that ostrich.

~

Tell your kids that giving flowers is just as satisfying as receiving them. Unless you are receiving them next to your casket at a funeral home.

~

Your daughter's missing purse is of great concern, but your son's missing purse is of far greater concern.

~

Inform your son that anything that lasts only a short time is not worth making a lifetime of sacrifices for. So he should break off the engagement to the stripper.

~

Tell your son that birds of a feather flock together. Then tell him that his friends are flocking assholes.

~

Advise your children that the greatest love always shows up unrepentantly, and sometimes in the most uncommon place, like the bathroom stall at the bus station.

~

Teach your child that to reach the top of the mountain he will need drive, determination, discipline, and a chairlift to carry his fat ass.

~

The moment your child is born, it's official. Your wife is now literally a Mother, and you are quite literally a Mother Fucker.

~

Watching a child fail is the most painful and necessary thing a parent can endure, except maybe natural child birth...no wait, that's not necessary.

~

Avoid naming your child "Simon" or you will have to do whatever he says.

～

Don't make the mistake of naming your child after his grandfather. "Grandpa" is a stupid name for a child.

～

A baby is somewhat of a miracle that comes out of a place that smells somewhat like a mackerel.

～

Hey Dad, you may not be the brightest person on earth, or the best looking — in fact, it's a certainty. That's all.

～

Tell your son that the early bird gets the worm, but the night owl gets the pussy.

TOOLS FOR
RAISING A TOOL

If you name your son Aaron, it's pretty clear that you didn't make it past page 1 in the baby name book.

~

In life, you're not always perfect on your first try. That's why your oldest child is usually a douche bag.

~

If your child is so goddamned special, why doesn't he ever get to eat off of the "good" dishes? Huh?

~

You are never too old for a pillow fight, but if you're over 90, try not to fracture your hip on the pillow.

~

When your children are arguing, tell them that two people can look at the same exact thing and see something totally different. This is particularly true when they have consumed hallucinogenic mushrooms.

~

A daughter is never too old to hug and kiss her father in public and, in Kentucky, a son is never too old to breast feed off of Mommy in public.

~

I cannot attend my child's music recital without a tissue in hand, because I'm allergic to terrible music.

~

Jesus loves the little children...except the ones named Judas...he hates them.

~

When your grandma says that you are beautiful on the inside, rest assured that you are hideously ugly on the outside.

~

Whoever said "you can't buy happiness" never bought a puppy, or hired a double-jointed Filipino hooker.

~

There is nothing about the caterpillar that tells you it's going to be a butterfly, and there is nothing about your child that tells you he is going to be a serial killer.

~

If a Little Leaguer wearing an eye patch is up at bat and he is not swinging, don't say "GOOD EYE!"

~

All parents take pride in watching their children grow up, except blind parents.

~

You should be grateful for all that you have, even if it isn't enough. You got that? You whiny starving African child! Look at all the flies you have.

~

If she is anything like her aunt, your little girl will graduate from playing house to playing whore house.

~

Little girls love rainbows. You should hang a rainbow flag outside of your home.

~

Assure your daughter that everyone makes mistakes — in fact, if it weren't for mistakes, she wouldn't exist.

~

Calm your nervous child by assuring him that having a cavity filled doesn't hurt, unless it's his anal cavity...then you're screwed.

~

The journey of 1000 miles begins with going pee pee in the potty because Daddy is not stopping.

~

Never say to your child with scoliosis, "Don't get all bent out of shape." That will hurt him, but not as much as the scoliosis.

~

Tell your children that unicorns really do exist, but only if a rhino screws a pony.

Hey Diddle Diddle, the Cat and the Fiddle...
Whoa, wait just a second.
Who the hell is diddling the cat? That's kitty porn, and it's wrong!
What's the matter? Cat got your tongue?

~

Tell your child that getting your name on the front page of the newspaper can be accomplished through hard work, dedication, or committing a heinous felony.

~

The more a child feels valued, the better his values will be, so start the bidding at $1000.

~

Sometimes, little things mean a lot...like the tiny granules of cocaine on your teenager's mirror.

~

Sad childhood memories can be erased with positive ones...or a serious head injury.

~

Warn your children that when they enter the Rat Race, they will be competing against their peers... other rats.

~

You should always do a background check on the people who are responsible for your child's safety...except the toothless, ex-con, carnival ride operator. He is probably OK.

~

If you give your child a lucky rabbit's foot, he will definitely smile, but if you hand him an entire dead rabbit on Easter Sunday, he will definitely cry.

~

It is simple math. No sun screen = red son screams.

~

Don't allow your son to drink milk directly out of the container. He may get crushed by the cow.

~

One day your daughter will be lying on the couch, and the next day she'll have the lead in the school play. A powerful piece of furniture — the Drama Teacher's Casting Couch.

~

A good father would never spank his Little Leaguer for striking out to end the game. A good father would instead, encourage his son by giving him a series of firm "high fives" against his buttocks.

~

Tell your teenager, it's better to give than to receive...an STD.

~

Honor thy mother, but don't get honor nerves.

~

When you buy your teenager his first car, make sure that it has cruise control. Cruise control is a drunk driver's best friend.

~

If your child gets something in his eye, gently remind him of the Tooth Fairy's cousin…"The Eye Ball Fairy."

~

If your teenager is into *Dungeons & Dragons*, rest assured, teen pregnancy will not be an issue of concern.

~

Advise your child to focus on the future because if you keep looking back, you'll eventually smash into something.

~

It's not a concern that your teenage son wears makeup. It is a concern that his clown name is "Junkie the Clown."

~

Tell your son that kindness is contagious, but so is chlamydia, so don't be kind to skanks.

~

Teach your daughter that she can only get ahead by working. Or twerking. Either one really.

~

A Bar Mitzvah is when a 13-year-old boy becomes...a wealthy 13-year-old boy.

~

Allow your son to establish his own identity, because the government will provide him with a new one right after he testifies.

~

If you want your child to smile, give him butterscotch. If you want your child to sleep, skip the butter and just go with Scotch.

DIRECTIONS TO FAMILY COURT

As a parent, sometimes your voice of reason has laryngitis.

~

Tell your child to follow her heart, unless her heart is in an Igloo cooler on the way to a transplant hospital. Then it's a moot point.

~

Let's be honest. Pinocchio was a liar, Aladdin was a thief, and Cinderella missed her curfew. Disney has shitty role models.

~

Tell your son that "people will judge you by your actions," and they are usually wearing long black robes and holding gavels when they do it.

~

Advise your grouchy son that if he turns his frown upside down, it becomes a smile. But if he turns his Elvis lip sneer upside down, it becomes a palsy.

~

Inside of every child is a spirit, or a tapeworm…or maybe the spirit of a tapeworm. Either way, you should get that checked out.

~

All children are temperamental. They lose their temper, and they go mental.

~

If your son has a stubborn loose tooth, tie a string around it and attach the other end of the string to the door handle…of your sports car. Then floor it. I assure you, the tooth will come out along with several pints of blood.

~

Teach your children to hum a tune when they are upset because it's impossible to sing with duct tape covering your mouth.

~

Tell your son that at one time, he was the fastest, strongest, and most determined swimmer out of millions of other sperm. He was victorious, and that's why he is here today. Then hit him with the reality that he will never reach that level of success again in his life. He peaked before he was born.

~

If the neighbor's dog growls at your children, toss his favorite fetching stick into a wood chipper. Technically, that's a suicide.

~

Childhood obesity is an epidemic. Be a role model for your kids, but not a cinnamon roll model.

～

Explain to your child that a Hershey's kiss is delicious, but a herpes kiss is malicious.

～

Advise your child that the best way to lose a friend is to lend him money. Be stingy, selfish and greedy, and you'll have lots of friends.

～

By the time a man realizes that his father was right, he has a son who thinks he is wrong. So send him to live with his know-it-all Grandpa.

～

When you are constantly arguing with your teenage son, you need to be the bigger man. Steroids should do the trick.

~

Level with your son, and if he still doesn't believe you, level him.

~

After about a week of watching your wife breast feed your son, it slowly seeps in. You had to buy her three fancy restaurant meals before she allowed you to do that. "This kid has to go."

~

When someone asks if your child has his grandfather's eyes, say, "Yes, thanks to the organ donor sticker on his license."

~

After your child is born, you'll be expected to know a bunch of stupid information like the birth weight, the length, the time of birth, and the who the father might be.

~

They say that, "A baby changes everything." You know what a baby doesn't change? His own diapers, and it's nasty. Welcome to hell.

~

Kids say the darndest things, but so do crack-heads, and the mentally ill. So if you know any crack-addicted, mentally ill kids, you should listen to them.

~

I tell my kids, "Every day, in every way you are getting better and better" but at the current rate, you won't be good enough until you are 70 years old, so let's pick it up a little.

~

Take it from me. When your child's school is holding a canned goods drive, a can of pipe tobacco will not be appreciated.

～

Some call it "Child Abandonment," but you can call it "Hide & Seek."

～

Treat all creepy male relatives like aspirin, and "Keep Away From Children."

～

If your child enjoys merry-go-rounds and the sensation of riding around in a circle, he is doomed to be a fan of NASCAR, and you have failed as a parent.

～

Children in the back seats of cars prevent accidents, but accidents in the back seats of cars cause children.

⁓

Children will repeat what you say, so remember to say, "Daddy has an enormous penis" at least twice a day.

⁓

To be in your children's memories tomorrow, you must be in their lives today...or in their nightmares. Either way is fine.

⁓

Play *Kick the Can*...as in Can-adian.

⁓

Give your children your undivided attention. Stalk them.

~

It's not only OK to lie to your children, it's recommended.

~

You will love your child's eyes, his smile, his tiny hands, and his soft little belly, but there will be days that you hate his guts.

~

Your child's greatest growth spurt will inevitably be the month after you've purchased expensive Nike sneakers.

~

You can't truly love a baby until you have a baby. But until you have a baby, you can hate all the babies you want to.

~

The sole purpose of a child's middle name is so he can tell when he's really in trouble.

~

To experience the joy of having grandchildren, you must first endure the emotional agony of having children.

~

Men are from Mars...women are from Venus... children are a pain in Uranus.

~

Species such as the Hyena, Wolf Spider, and Polar Bear all eat their young…I'm just saying.

~

Instead of telling your child to put on his socks and shoes, simplify it by saying, "Get your feet dressed." It's both cute and confusing.

~

Some dads play *Hide & Seek* with their kids, and the really good ones aren't found until the kids reach adulthood.

~

You will want your children to have everything you had as a child. Good luck finding a Lite Brite.

~

Tell your son that he could make a fortune off of the tooth fairy if he keeps talking back to Daddy.

THE FRUIT OF YOUR LOINS IS ROTTEN

Eagles do not allow their offspring to return to the nest once they leave. Soar like an eagle.

~๑

It's hard to teach your children about tolerance when you are drinking lactose-free milk.

~๑

"Childhood" is a great name for juvenile foreskin.

~๑

Occasionally give your child a pat on the back…especially when he is choking on a chicken bone.

~๑

Warn your child that when push comes to shove, a punch in the face is probably next.

~

Teach your kids to be selective when choosing their friends. For example, no bullies, no cheaters, and no Hungarians.

~

You are your son's moral compass and, for that reason, he should invest in a GPS.

~

Teach your child that beggars can't be choosers, but they can be losers, boozers, and abusers.

~

Remind your child that Popeye ate a lot of spinach, but he also smoked a pipe, and who's to say that the pipe didn't make him stronger?

~

Allow your child to watch the television for two hours each day, but never plug it in.

~

If your son breaks a window, he should pay to have it repaired. If your daughter breaks a mirror, you should pay for her nose job.

~

If your teenage son uses the argument that the Rothsteins are letting their son go to the concert, casually mention what the Rothsteins did to their son's penis shortly after he was born.

~

If your 12-year-old daughter wants to start wearing makeup, tell her she has your permission, as long as it is clown makeup, and she has to be wearing really big shoes.

~

Rome wasn't built in a day, but you made little Tommy in just under 4 minutes.

~

A bomb shelter with lead walls is the safest place to be during a nuclear attack, so lead paint on the nursery walls is actually a very good idea.

~

Pregnancy. It happens even in the best of families.

~

Tell your children that money doesn't grow on trees. It does however get stuck in Mommy's G-string when she is at work. So while it may not grow on trees, it can be found in bushes.

~

They grow up so fast. One day she is sprinkling Fairy Dust and the next day she is smoking Angel Dust.

~

Tell your son to aim high. That way he is less likely to pee on his shoes.

~

It takes a whole village to raise a child, but one child can burn down a whole village.

~

When your child asks what the future holds, don't lead off with a fat, nagging wife and a soul crushing job.

~

Tell your son that it's OK to play with dolls as long as they are Voodoo dolls.

~

If you want your kids to be down-to-earth, over-feed them. Gravity is kind to the morbidly obese.

~

Give your kids ice cream, so they will like you better.

~

It's Prom night. Spring is in the air — and it's a good bet that your daughter's ankles are, too.

~

If your son inquires about "hormones," it's best to tell him the truth. If a whore moans, she is probably faking it.

~

Warn your son that an education is something that no one can take away from you. They can, however take your home and your car when you default on your student loans.

~

Impress upon your son that it won't kill him to make his bed each morning, but it might kill him if he doesn't. "It", by the way, is you.

~

Your children are the next generation. Did you ever notice that the word "generation" has the word "RAT" in the middle of it?

~

Children are the fabric of our society. Fabric that is stained with drool, urine, vomit, and poo.

~

Tell your child that you'll give him something to cry about, and then make him watch *Brian's Song*.

~

Light travels faster than sound, so your child will appear to be bright, until he opens his mouth.

~

It's a parent's duty to clean his child's booty, while not getting cooties from the nudie, booty duty.

~

When your child is not eating, place him in the high chair, which is any chair as long as he is high. His appetite will come around.

~

So your little angel is a thumb sucker. Big deal. It's both natural, and normal. It's also a skill and a talent that will make her very popular in college.

~

When your child won't stop crying I recommend a bottle. Smash it on the curb and then menace him with the jagged end. He'll shut up.

~

There is a good reason why babies can't speak. They are very cranky, and they have nothing nice to say.

~

Baptize your child, not for religious reasons but rather to show him how easy it would be to drown him.

~

Your child must learn that you "don't cry over spilled milk, unless it is spilling out of bullet holes in Mommy's breasts."

~

Tell your child, "You get what you get, and you don't get upset" — unless you are waiting for a heart transplant and they accidentally give you a liver. Then, by all means, get upset.

~

Inform your child that "nice manners will get you nice things" but so will incriminating photos of powerful people.

~

Warn your child that "Big Brother is watching," so he should spackle that peep hole and tell Mom.

~

Son, you may do something in an instant that you may regret for a lifetime. Knocking up Mommy comes instantly to mind.

~

Accept the fact that some days you're the pigeon, and some days you're the statue. If you are a statue of a pigeon however, then God just hates you.

~

Even if you "child proof" your home,
they will find a way to get in.